Pro-Course For Marketing Automation

*Leveraging Tools to Streamline
Campaigns and Boost Efficiency*

Aziza Tawfiq Abdelghafar

DEDICATION

For those who dare to dream, persist through challenges, and embrace the journey of lifelong learning. Your resilience shapes the future.

Table of contents

ACKNOWLEDGMENTS

I am deeply grateful to everyone who played a role in bringing this book to life. To my family, whose unwavering support fuels my ambition; to my friends, who inspire and challenge me; and to my mentors and colleagues, whose insights and wisdom have guided my path. Your encouragement has been invaluable.

Thank you for believing in this journey.

About the Book

Marketing is evolving fast, and keeping up requires more than just creativity—it demands efficiency. That's where automation comes in. *Pro-Course for Marketing Automation: Leveraging Tools to Streamline Campaigns and Boost Efficiency* is your hands-on guide to mastering the tools and strategies that save time, cut costs, and maximize results.

This book isn't just theory. It's a practical roadmap packed with real-world applications, from email workflows to social media bots and AI-driven ad campaigns. Whether you're a solo marketer, a business owner, or part of a team, you'll learn how to automate repetitive tasks, personalize customer journeys, and turn data into smarter decisions.

Inside, you'll find step-by-step tutorials, tool comparisons, and ready-to-use templates—all designed to help you implement automation quickly and effectively. By the end, you'll be equipped to design campaigns that run like clockwork, giving you more room to focus on strategy and growth.

Preface

Let's be honest: marketing today is a mix of endless tasks — emails, ads, social posts, analytics — and trying to juggle it all manually is exhausting. But what if you could automate the repetitive stuff while making your campaigns *more* effective? That's the power of marketing automation, and this book is your shortcut to making it work for you.

I wrote this guide because I've seen too many talented marketers burn out on busywork or miss opportunities because they're stuck in the weeds. Automation isn't about replacing creativity; it's about freeing up your time *for* creativity. Whether you're new to tools like HubSpot or Mailchimp or you're looking to level up your existing workflows, this book breaks things down in plain English, with no fluff or confusing jargon.

Each chapter builds on real scenarios — recovering abandoned carts, scheduling social posts, optimizing ads with AI — and includes practical tasks so you can apply what you learn immediately. The goal? To help you work smarter, not harder.

So, if you're ready to transform how you do marketing (and maybe reclaim a few hours in your week), let's dive in. The future of efficient, scalable campaigns starts here.

Course Introduction

Marketing automation might sound like just another buzzword, but it's actually one of the most practical ways to make your marketing efforts smoother, faster, and more effective. Think of it like putting certain tasks on autopilot—emails that send themselves, ads that adjust bids based on performance, or social media posts that go live at the perfect time without you lifting a finger. But it's not just about saving time. It's about working smarter so you can focus on the big-picture strategies that really move the needle for your business.

So what exactly does marketing automation mean? At its core, it's using software to handle repetitive marketing tasks that would otherwise eat up your day. Instead of manually sending follow-up emails to every new subscriber or posting on five different social platforms at odd hours, automation tools let you set up rules and workflows once, then let the system do the heavy lifting. This doesn't mean your marketing becomes impersonal—quite the opposite. With the right setup, automation lets you deliver more timely, relevant, and personalized experiences to your audience, which is something customers have come to expect these days.

Now, how does this actually improve efficiency and cut costs? Well, time is money, especially in marketing. When you automate routine tasks, you free up hours in your week—hours you'd otherwise spend on tedious, repetitive work. That means your team can focus on creative campaigns, strategy, or engaging directly with customers instead of getting bogged down in administrative details. Automation also reduces human error. No more accidentally sending the wrong email to the wrong list or forgetting to schedule a critical post. Plus, many automation tools come with analytics built in, so you can see what's working and what's not in real time, allowing you to tweak campaigns on the fly without wasting budget on underperforming ads or emails.

The benefits of automation in today's marketing landscape are hard to ignore. For starters, it helps you stay consistent. Whether it's email sequences, social media updates, or ad placements, automation ensures your messaging stays on track even when you're busy with other things. It also scales with your business. What works for 100 customers will work just as smoothly for 10,000—without requiring 100 times the effort. And let's not forget personalization. Modern consumers don't just tolerate personalized marketing; they expect it. Automation tools let you segment audiences, tailor messages, and trigger actions based on user behavior, making your campaigns feel more relevant and engaging.

This course is designed for anyone who wants to work smarter, not harder. If you're a marketer tired of drowning in repetitive tasks, an entrepreneur wearing too many hats, or part of a marketing team looking to streamline operations, you'll find value here. Maybe you're already using basic tools like Mailchimp or Hootsuite but want to take your automation game to the next level. Or perhaps you're completely new to the idea and need a clear, no-fluff guide to get started. Wherever you fall on that spectrum, this course will give you the practical know-how to implement automation in a way that makes sense for your goals.

The bottom line? Marketing automation isn't about replacing the human touch—it's about enhancing it. By letting technology handle the repetitive stuff, you can focus on what really matters: building relationships, crafting compelling messages, and growing your business. And that's exactly what we'll explore together in this course. So if you're ready to ditch the busywork and make your marketing more efficient, let's dive in.

Unit 1: Fundamentals of Marketing Automation

Let's be real—marketing isn't what it used to be. Gone are the days when you could manually send emails to every customer or post on social media whenever you remembered. Today, if you're not working smart, you're just working hard. That's where marketing automation comes in, and this unit is your starting point to understanding how it can transform the way you do business.

Marketing automation might sound technical, but at its heart, it's about making your life easier. Imagine having a virtual assistant that handles all those repetitive tasks—sending follow-up emails, posting content at the right time, even nudging customers who left items in their cart. Sounds good, right? But before we dive into the how, let's get clear on the what. What exactly is marketing automation, and how is it different from the old-school way of doing things?

We'll break it down in simple terms—no jargon, just straight talk about how automation works and why it's a game-changer. You'll learn how it saves you time (because who doesn't want more of that?), boosts your results, and even makes your customers happier by delivering the right message at the right time. And because tools are what make automation possible, we'll walk through some of the most popular ones—Mailchimp, HubSpot, ActiveCampaign—and help you figure out which might be the best fit for your needs.

By the end of this unit, you won't just understand marketing automation—you'll be ready to take it for a test drive. Your first practical task? Pick a tool, poke around its interface, and start getting comfortable with how it works. Consider it your first step toward working smarter, not harder. So let's get started—your future self (the one with more free time and better results) will thank you.

Lesson 1: What is Marketing Automation?

Let's cut through the noise and talk about what marketing automation really means in the real world. Picture this: you're a small business owner who's been manually sending emails to every new subscriber, posting on social media whenever you remember, and trying to keep track of customers who showed interest but didn't buy. It's exhausting, right? That's where marketing automation comes in - it's like having a digital assistant that handles all those repetitive tasks while you focus on growing your business.

At its core, marketing automation is about using software to handle routine marketing tasks automatically. But it's so much more than just scheduling emails. Think of it as setting up intelligent workflows that respond to your customers' actions. When someone signs up for your newsletter? They automatically get a welcome series. When a customer abandons their cart? They receive a gentle reminder. When a lead hasn't engaged in a while? The system nudges them with relevant content. All of this happens without you having to manually trigger each action.

The magic happens through triggers and workflows. A trigger could be anything - a website visit, a form submission, a purchase, or even inactivity. The workflow is what happens next - the series of automated actions that guide the customer through their journey with your brand. This isn't about replacing human interaction - it's about enhancing it by making sure the right message reaches the right person at the right time.

Now let's talk about how this differs from traditional marketing. Remember when marketing meant blasting the same message to everyone on your list and hoping it worked? Automation turns that approach on its head. Instead of one-size-fits-all campaigns, you're creating personalized experiences at scale. Where traditional marketing reacts, automation anticipates. Where manual processes are inconsistent, automation delivers reliability. And while old-school methods often mean working harder as you grow, automation actually makes scaling easier.

The tools available today make this accessible to businesses of all sizes. On the simpler end, you've got platforms like Mailchimp that handle email automation beautifully. Then there's more comprehensive solutions like HubSpot that manage everything from emails to social media to lead scoring. ActiveCampaign strikes a great balance with powerful automation features that don't overwhelm beginners. And that's just scratching the surface - there are specialized tools for every aspect of marketing automation you can imagine.

What's fascinating is how these tools have evolved. Early marketing automation was clunky and obvious - customers could tell they were getting generic automated messages. Today's tools use AI and machine learning to create experiences that feel personal and timely. They can analyze customer behavior to predict what content someone might need next, or automatically adjust email send times for maximum open rates.

But here's the thing about automation tools - they're only as good as the strategy behind them. The real power comes from understanding your customer journey and mapping out how automation can enhance that experience. It's not about automating everything possible, but about identifying the repetitive tasks that eat up your time and the touchpoints where personalization matters most.

One of the biggest mindset shifts with marketing automation is moving from campaign thinking to journey thinking. Instead of focusing on individual emails or social posts, you're designing an entire experience that guides potential customers from first awareness through to purchase and beyond. This approach creates more cohesive messaging and better results over time.

The beauty of modern marketing automation is that it's no longer just for big corporations with massive budgets. Cloud-based tools have democratized these capabilities, putting powerful automation within reach of solopreneurs and small teams. You don't need a technical background to get started - most platforms use intuitive drag-and-drop interfaces that make setting up workflows surprisingly simple.

What often surprises people is how automation can actually make marketing feel more human, not less. When you automate the routine stuff, you free up time for genuine human connection where it matters most. Instead of spending hours scheduling social posts, you can have real conversations in the comments. Rather than manually sending follow-up emails, you can focus on crafting messages that truly resonate.

The key is to start small and build as you go. Maybe begin with automating your welcome emails, then add abandoned cart sequences, then explore more advanced segmentation. Each step builds on the last, creating a system that works harder for you over time. And the data you collect through these automated interactions becomes invaluable for understanding your audience and refining your approach.

At the end of the day, marketing automation isn't about setting up technology and walking away. It's about creating systems that allow you to market smarter - with more consistency, more personalization, and better results. It's the difference between working in your business and working on your business. And in today's competitive landscape, that difference can be everything.

Lesson 2: Why Should You Use Marketing Automation?

Let me tell you a story about my friend Sarah who runs an online boutique. She was spending hours every day sending individual follow-up emails, posting on social media, and trying to keep up with customer inquiries. Then she discovered marketing automation. Within weeks, she reclaimed 15 hours a week while seeing better results than ever before. That's the power we're talking about here - working smarter, not harder.

The time-saving benefits alone make automation worth considering. Think about all those repetitive tasks that eat up your day - sending welcome emails, posting content across multiple platforms, following up with leads. Automation handles these while you sleep. One ecommerce store owner told me he used to spend every Monday morning manually sending abandoned cart emails. Now his system automatically sends a series of three emails with personalized product recommendations, recovering 18% of would-be lost sales without him lifting a finger.

But saving time is just the beginning. Where automation really shines is in enhancing your marketing performance. Here's why: consistency and precision. Manual processes inevitably lead to gaps - maybe you forget to send a follow-up or post inconsistently. Automation ensures every customer gets the right message at the right time, every time. A/B testing becomes effortless too - you can automatically send different email versions to segments of your list and let the system determine the winner.

The performance boost comes from data-driven decisions. Automation tools track everything - open rates, click patterns, conversion paths. You start seeing what actually works rather than guessing. One consultant client of mine discovered through automation data that her mid-week educational emails performed 37% better than promotional Friday emails - something she never would have spotted manually.

Now let's talk about the customer experience, because this is where automation truly transforms your marketing from good to great. Today's consumers expect personalized, relevant interactions. They want you to remember their preferences and anticipate their needs. Trying to deliver this manually is impossible beyond a handful of customers. Automation makes personalization at scale achievable.

Imagine a new subscriber who downloads your lead magnet about keto dieting. With automation, they automatically get a welcome sequence about keto, then later receive recipe ideas and product recommendations tailored to their interests. If they click on dessert recipes but ignore breakfast ideas, the system adjusts what it sends next. This creates a customer journey that feels bespoke, not generic.

The experience extends beyond just emails. Chatbots can provide instant answers to common questions at 2 AM when your team's asleep. Dynamic website content can change based on visitor behavior. Retargeting ads can automatically show products similar to what someone browsed. All these automated touchpoints create a cohesive, personalized experience that builds trust and loyalty.

What's fascinating is how automation actually enables more human connections, not fewer. By handling routine interactions automatically, you free up time and mental space for genuine relationship-building where it matters most. Instead of rushing through customer service replies to keep up, your team can focus on complex issues requiring empathy and creativity. Rather than spending all day scheduling posts, you can engage in meaningful social media conversations.

The financial impact is hard to ignore too. While there's an initial investment in tools and setup, the long-term savings are substantial. One study found businesses using marketing automation see an average 12% reduction in marketing overhead. More importantly, they see a 14.5% increase in sales productivity. That's because your team stops being administrative assistants and starts being strategic marketers.

Lead nurturing becomes particularly powerful with automation. Instead of letting promising leads go cold because someone forgot to follow up, automated workflows ensure every lead gets timely, relevant content moving them toward a purchase. One B2B company increased their sales-qualified leads by 45% simply by implementing automated lead scoring and nurturing.

There's also the competitive advantage to consider. As more businesses adopt automation, customer expectations rise. They're getting used to instant responses, personalized recommendations, and seamless experiences. If you're still doing everything manually, you're not just working harder - you're falling behind. Early adopters of automation consistently outperform competitors who rely on manual processes.

Scalability is another game-changer. Manual processes that work fine with 100 customers become unsustainable at 1,000. Automation grows with your business. The same workflows that nurture 10 leads can nurture 10,000 without additional effort. This removes one of the biggest barriers to growth many small businesses face.

Let's not overlook the stress reduction factor too. Marketing is stressful enough without worrying whether you remembered to send that important email sequence or post today's content. Automation creates peace of mind knowing the system has your back. One entrepreneur told me implementing automation was like "getting rid of that constant nagging feeling I was forgetting something important."

The data insights automation provides are invaluable for continuous improvement. Instead of guessing what works, you have clear metrics showing which messages resonate, which offers convert, and where prospects drop off. This allows for constant optimization - tweaking subject lines here, adjusting send times there, refining workflows based on actual behavior rather than hunches.

Perhaps most importantly, automation gives you back something priceless: focus. Instead of jumping between a dozen small tasks, you can concentrate on big-picture strategy, creative campaigns, and business growth. The mental shift from "how will I get all this done?" to "how can we improve results?" is transformative for many business owners and marketers.

The beauty is you don't need to automate everything at once. Start with your biggest pain points - maybe that's email follow-ups or social media scheduling. As you see results and gain confidence, you can expand to more sophisticated automations. The key is to begin where automation will make the most immediate impact on your time, performance, or customer experience.

At its core, marketing automation isn't about replacing human marketers but empowering them. It handles the repetitive so you can focus on the remarkable. It ensures consistency while enabling personalization. It provides data to inform better decisions. In today's fast-paced digital landscape, it's not just a nice-to-have - it's becoming essential for businesses that want to compete and thrive.

Lesson 3: Popular Marketing Automation Tools

Picture this: you walk into a hardware store needing to fix a leaky pipe. There are dozens of wrenches on the wall - some basic, some fancy, some you don't even recognize. Choosing the right one makes your job easy. Pick wrong, and you'll just frustrate yourself. Marketing automation tools work the same way. Today we're going to explore three of the most popular options - Mailchimp, HubSpot, and ActiveCampaign - to help you find the perfect fit for your business needs.

Let's start with Mailchimp, the friendly neighborhood option that many small businesses fall in love with first. Remember when Mailchimp was just an email service? Those days are long gone. Today it's grown into a full-fledged marketing platform while keeping its signature user-friendly approach. What makes Mailchimp special is how it holds your hand through the automation process. Setting up your first automated welcome series feels like following a recipe - simple, step-by-step, with clear instructions. Their visual workflow builder uses colorful blocks and intuitive drag-and-drop controls that make complex automation feel approachable. For the solopreneur or small team just dipping toes into automation, this can be a game-changer. Their free plan lets you manage up to 500 contacts, which is perfect for testing the waters without financial commitment. Where Mailchimp really shines is in ecommerce integrations - hook it up to your Shopify or WooCommerce store, and suddenly you're sending personalized product recommendations and abandoned cart emails like a pro. The reporting is beautifully visual too, showing you exactly how your automations are performing at a glance. But there's a trade-off for all that simplicity. When your needs grow more sophisticated - say you want to score leads based on multiple behaviors or create branching conditional workflows - you might find Mailchimp's capabilities starting to feel a bit limited. It's like outgrowing training wheels - wonderful when you're starting, but eventually you'll want more control.

Now let's talk about HubSpot, the Swiss Army knife of marketing automation. If Mailchimp is your friendly local hardware store, HubSpot is the massive home improvement warehouse with every tool imaginable. Their free CRM forms the foundation, seamlessly connecting with their marketing, sales, and service hubs. What sets HubSpot apart is how everything talks to each other - a contact's email engagement data informs the sales team's outreach which then triggers customer service follow-ups, all in one ecosystem. Their automation builder is incredibly powerful yet remains surprisingly accessible, using a flowchart-style interface that helps you visualize customer journeys. Lead scoring works beautifully here - you can assign points for email opens, website visits, form submissions, then automatically notify sales when someone hits your threshold. The reporting is enterprise-grade too, letting you track ROI across entire campaigns and customer lifecycles. HubSpot really shines for B2B companies or any business with a complex sales cycle. Their sequences tool lets you automate multi-channel nurture campaigns that mix emails, tasks, and ads based on how prospects engage. But all this power comes with a steeper learning curve, and pricing can escalate quickly as you add contacts and premium features. It's worth noting their free tools are remarkably generous though - you can accomplish quite a bit before needing to upgrade.

ActiveCampaign sits in that sweet spot between Mailchimp's simplicity and HubSpot's comprehensiveness. Think of it as the specialist's tool - laser-focused on delivering incredibly sophisticated automation through an interface that remains approachable. Their automation builder is arguably the most flexible of the three, allowing for intricate conditional logic that can respond to dozens of customer behaviors and data points. What makes ActiveCampaign special is how it combines email marketing, CRM, and automation into one seamless flow. Their site tracking features are particularly impressive - you can trigger automations based on specific pages visited, time spent on site, or even inactivity. The segmentation is next-level too, letting you slice your audience by virtually any criteria then personalize messaging accordingly. Sales automation features like deal pipelines and win probabilities make it a great choice for businesses that need to bridge marketing and sales. The reporting provides deep insights into how each automation impacts revenue, not just opens and clicks. While the interface isn't as instantly intuitive as Mailchimp's, ActiveCampaign offers excellent onboarding resources to get you up to speed. Pricing is middle-of-the-road - more than Mailchimp's entry levels but often more affordable than HubSpot for comparable features. Where it might fall short is if you need robust social media or ads management baked in - you'll likely need to connect other tools for those functions.

Now that we've met our three contenders, how do you choose? It comes down to understanding your business's unique needs and growth trajectory. Mailchimp is your best bet if you want something you can start using today with minimal setup, especially for basic email automation and ecommerce. The trade-off is less flexibility as your needs grow more complex. HubSpot makes the most sense when you need an all-in-one platform that can scale with your business across marketing, sales, and service - just be prepared for the learning curve and potential cost as you expand. ActiveCampaign hits that middle ground beautifully - powerful enough for sophisticated automation yet focused enough to avoid feeling overwhelming, ideal for businesses that want deep customer journey automation without the full suite of HubSpot features.

Beyond these big three, there's a whole ecosystem of specialized tools worth mentioning briefly. ConvertKit is fantastic for creators and bloggers with its visual automation builder and focus on audience segments. Drip shines for ecommerce with its robust product-based workflows. Keap (formerly Infusionsoft) caters beautifully to service businesses with its strong CRM integration. Marketo serves enterprise needs with incredibly complex automation capabilities. Each has its strengths, but our focus today remains on the three most versatile options suitable for most small to midsize businesses.

Implementation is where many businesses stumble, regardless of which tool they choose. The biggest mistake? Trying to automate everything at once. Start small - maybe just your welcome series and abandoned cart flows. Get comfortable with how triggers and actions work. Watch how your audience responds. Then gradually add more sophisticated automations as you gain confidence. Most platforms offer templates and pre-built workflows that can give you a head start - use them! Another common pitfall is setting and forgetting. Automation isn't fire-and-forget - you need to regularly review performance data and tweak your flows. Maybe that abandoned cart email performs better when sent after 6 hours rather than 24. Perhaps your welcome series has too many emails causing unsubscribes. The tools provide the data - you provide the human insight to optimize.

Integration capabilities should weigh heavily in your decision too. Check how well each platform plays with your existing tech stack - your ecommerce platform, CRM, webinar software, etc. HubSpot typically leads here with its vast integration library, but both Mailchimp and ActiveCampaign connect with most major platforms through native integrations or Zapier. Mobile experience matters more than many realize too - if you or your team need to monitor or adjust automations on the go, test each platform's mobile app before committing.

Pricing structures vary significantly between these tools, and it's not always apples-to-apples comparison. Mailchimp charges primarily based on contact count. HubSpot uses a tiered feature approach across its hubs. ActiveCampaign blends contact count with feature levels. Watch out for hidden costs like charges for additional users or premium support. Most offer free trials or freemium versions - use these extensively before committing. Nothing beats hands-on experience for understanding which interface and workflow makes most sense for how your brain works.

The human element remains crucial regardless of which tool you choose. Automation works best when it enhances rather than replaces genuine human connection. Use these tools to handle the repetitive tasks so you can focus on creative strategy and personal interactions where they matter most. The right tool feels like an extension of your team, not a robotic overlord. It should make your marketing feel more human, not less.

Looking ahead, all these platforms are rapidly incorporating AI features to make automation even smarter - predictive sending times, content suggestions, even generative AI for email copy. While exciting, remember the fundamentals matter most. No amount of AI magic will save poorly planned automations. Focus first on understanding your customer journey, mapping key touchpoints, and identifying where automation can add genuine value. The tools are just that - tools. Your strategy and creativity remain the secret sauce.

As we wrap up, remember that choosing a marketing automation platform isn't a marriage - it's okay to start with one and migrate as your needs change. Many businesses begin with Mailchimp for its simplicity, then graduate to ActiveCampaign or HubSpot as their requirements grow more sophisticated. The important thing is to start somewhere. Pick one that feels comfortable for your current needs and skill level, then dive in. The practical task for this lesson - exploring one tool's interface - is designed to give you that hands-on feel before committing. Trust me, within an hour of playing with the automation builder in any of these platforms, you'll start seeing possibilities you never imagined for streamlining your marketing and delighting your customers. That moment when your first automated campaign goes live and starts delivering results while you sleep? That's the magic we're working toward.

Practical Task: Hands-On With Marketing Automation

Now that we've covered the basics, it's time to roll up your sleeves and get familiar with one of these tools. Think of this like test-driving a car—you don't need to be an expert mechanic to get a feel for how it handles.

Your Mission (If You Choose to Accept It):

Pick **one** marketing automation tool—Mailchimp, HubSpot, or ActiveCampaign—and spend 30-60 minutes exploring its dashboard. No pressure to build anything fancy yet. Just click around, see what's where, and get comfortable with the interface.

How to Get Started:

1. **Sign Up for a Free Account**

   o All three platforms offer free tiers or trials.

   o *Mailchimp*: Great if you want something simple and visual.

   o *HubSpot*: Ideal if you want CRM + marketing tools together.

   o *ActiveCampaign*: Best if you love detailed automation workflows.

2. **Take a Quick Tour**

   o Most tools have an onboarding walkthrough — don't skip it!

   o Look for:

   ▪ **Email Campaign Builder** (How do you create one?)

   ▪ **Automation Workflows** (Can you find the "if-this-then-that" triggers?)

   ▪ **Contact/List Management** (How does it organize your audience?)

   ▪ **Reports/Analytics** (Where do you check performance?)

3. **Try One Small Thing**

   o In *Mailchimp*: Set up a basic welcome email for new subscribers.

   o In *HubSpot*: Create a simple lead-nurturing sequence.

   o In *ActiveCampaign*: Build a two-step automation (e.g., "If someone opens Email A, send Email B").

4. **Ask Yourself:**

- ○ Does the layout feel intuitive, or does it make you want to pull your hair out?

- ○ Can you see yourself using this daily, or does it feel overwhelming?

- ○ Bonus: Take screenshots of anything confusing or exciting — you'll want to remember it later.

Why This Matters

Tools are like shoes — what works for someone else might pinch your toes. This quick test helps you:

- **Avoid buyer's remorse** (no one wants to pay for software they hate using).

- **Spot the right fit early** (some tools just "click" with how you think).

- **Build confidence** (automation feels less scary once you've poked around).

Pro Tip:

If you're stuck, search "[Tool Name] + beginner tutorial" on YouTube. A 10-minute video can save you hours of frustration.

Ready? Go play! Come back when you've got a feel for one tool — we'll build on this in the next lessons. 🚀

Note: No perfect choice exists — just the best one for YOU right now. Trust your gut!

Unit 2: Email Marketing Automation

Let's talk about email—the workhorse of digital marketing. You might think email is old school in the age of TikTok and chatbots, but here's the truth: it still delivers one of the highest returns of any marketing channel. The catch? Doing it manually is exhausting. That's where automation comes in.

Imagine this: instead of sending every welcome email by hand, chasing down abandoned carts one by one, or trying to remember who needs a product reminder, you set up smart systems that handle all of this for you—while you sleep. That's what we're diving into in this unit.

Email automation isn't about spamming inboxes with generic blasts. It's about creating timely, relevant conversations with your audience without burning yourself out. We'll cover everything from basic welcome sequences (those "Thanks for signing up!" emails that actually get opened) to more advanced behavioral triggers (like sending a special offer to someone who keeps eyeing a product but hasn't bought).

You'll learn how to rescue abandoned carts (because yes, those "Forgot something?" emails really do work), how to segment your lists so your messages feel personal, and how to track what's actually working so you can stop guessing and start improving.

By the end, you'll set up your first automated campaign—something you can use right away, whether you're selling products, services, or just building an audience. The best part? Once it's set up, it keeps working for you. No more last-minute scrambles to send promotions or follow-ups. Just consistent, effective emails that build relationships (and sales) while you focus on the bigger picture.

Ready to turn your inbox into your hardest-working employee? Let's get started.

Lesson 1: Creating Automated Email Campaigns

Let me tell you about Sarah, who runs a small online jewelry store. She used to spend hours every week manually sending emails to new subscribers, following up with customers who left items in their carts, and announcing new collections. Then she discovered automated email campaigns. Within a month, her sales increased by 30% while she actually worked fewer hours. That's the power we're about to unlock for you.

Automated email campaigns aren't about blasting generic messages to your entire list. They're about having thoughtful, timely conversations with your customers at scale. Think of it like setting up dominoes - you carefully arrange them once, then watch as each action triggers the next perfect move. The best part? These campaigns work while you sleep, take vacations, or focus on other parts of your business.

Welcome Series: Your Digital Handshake

That first email someone gets after signing up? It's more important than you might think. A well-crafted welcome series can generate up to 50% more engagement than regular newsletters. But here's what most businesses get wrong - they send just one "thanks for subscribing" message and call it done.

A true welcome sequence is a conversation starter. The first email might thank them and set expectations ("You'll get weekly styling tips every Tuesday"). The second could introduce your brand story ("How I went from making jewelry at my kitchen table to running this business"). The third might offer a special first-purchase discount. Each email builds trust and familiarity, making that first purchase much more likely.

Timing matters too. That first email should hit inboxes within minutes of signing up - when excitement is highest. Then space the next messages a few days apart. Tools like Mailchimp and ActiveCampaign make this easy with their visual workflow builders where you can literally drag and drop emails into a timeline.

Abandoned Cart Reminders: Your Silent Sales Team

Here's a staggering statistic - about 70% of online shopping carts get abandoned. But here's the good news: well-timed automated reminders can recover 10-30% of those lost sales. The key is in the approach.

Your first reminder (sent within 1-2 hours) might gently say, "Forgot something? Your cart is waiting!" The second (24 hours later) could address common objections ("Free shipping on all orders over $50"). The final one (48 hours out) might create urgency ("Only 2 left in stock!").

The most effective abandoned cart emails include images of the abandoned items, clear CTAs, and sometimes even personalized discounts. Most ecommerce platforms like Shopify integrate directly with email tools to make these automations a breeze to set up.

Product Launch Sequences: Building Anticipation

Remember how Apple creates buzz before new product releases? You can use the same principle on a smaller scale with automated launch sequences. Start teasing your new product 2-3 weeks out with behind-the-scenes content ("Meet the designer creating our new collection").

As launch day approaches, increase the frequency and urgency ("Only 3 days until our biggest sale of the year!"). Post-launch, follow up with social proof ("See what our first customers are saying!"). This structured approach consistently outperforms one-off "now available" announcements.

Behavioral Triggers: The Secret Sauce

This is where automation gets really powerful. Instead of sending the same emails to everyone, you can trigger messages based on how people interact with your previous emails or website.

Did someone click on your "winter coats" link but not buy? Two days later they might get an email with coat styling tips. Did they open your last three emails but not click anything? They might get a different message than someone who hasn't opened anything in a month.

Tools like ActiveCampaign and HubSpot let you set up these "if this, then that" rules visually. For example: "IF customer clicks on 'red dresses' BUT doesn't purchase WITHIN 3 days, THEN send red dress styling guide."

Personalization Beyond "Hi [First Name]"

While addressing people by name is nice, true personalization goes deeper. You can automatically include:

- Products they've viewed but didn't buy

- Items that complement their past purchases

- Location-specific content ("Come visit our Chicago store!")

- Milestones ("Happy 1-year anniversary as a customer!")

Most email platforms pull this data from your website or CRM. The result? Emails that feel like they were handcrafted for each recipient, even though you set up the template once.

Testing and Optimization

Here's the thing about email automation - your first version won't be perfect, and that's okay. The beauty is you can test and improve over time. Try different subject lines for your welcome email. Experiment with sending your abandoned cart sequence at different intervals. Most tools provide detailed analytics showing what's working.

A/B testing (sending two variations to see which performs better) is built into most platforms. You might discover that your audience prefers emojis in subject lines, or that sending reminder emails in the evening gets more clicks. These small optimizations compound into significant results over time.

Common Pitfalls to Avoid

Even with the best tools, some mistakes can sabotage your automated campaigns:

- Setting and forgetting (always review performance monthly)

- Over-automating (some situations still need human touch)

- Not cleaning your lists (remove inactive subscribers regularly)

- Ignoring mobile optimization (most emails are read on phones)

The most successful automated email programs strike a balance between systemized efficiency and human authenticity. Your emails should sound like they're coming from a real person (because they are), just amplified by technology.

As you start building your first campaigns, remember this isn't about perfection. Start simple - maybe just a 3-email welcome sequence. Get comfortable with that, then add more sophisticated automations. Within a few months, you'll have an entire ecosystem of emails working together to nurture relationships and drive sales, all while you focus on growing your business in other ways.

That's the real magic of email automation - it lets you be everywhere at once, having meaningful conversations with hundreds or thousands of customers simultaneously, in a way that feels personal and authentic. And that's a superpower worth developing.

Lesson 2: Handling Abandoned Carts

Picture this: A customer spends twenty minutes browsing your online store, carefully selects items worth $150, gets all the way to checkout... then vanishes. Poof. Gone. It happens to every ecommerce business—about 70% of online shopping carts get abandoned before purchase. But here's the good news: with the right automated strategy, you can recover a significant chunk of those would-be lost sales while you sleep.

Why Carts Get Abandoned (And How to Fix It)

Before we dive into automation, let's understand why people bail at the last second. Common reasons include:

- **Unexpected costs** (shipping fees, taxes)

- **Just browsing** (not ready to buy yet)

- **Checkout process too complicated**

- **Website performance issues**

- **Comparison shopping**

Your abandoned cart emails should address these pain points. The best ones don't just say "You forgot something!"—they remove friction and add value.

The Three-Email Recovery Sequence That Works

Most successful stores use a sequence of 2-3 automated emails, each with a distinct purpose:

Email 1: The Gentle Reminder

Sent within 1-2 hours of abandonment

Subject line: "Your cart is getting lonely!" or "Did you forget something?"

Content: Show the abandoned items with clear images, include a prominent CTA button, and briefly restate your value proposition (free returns, secure checkout, etc.).

Pro tip: Add social proof like "5 people viewed this item today" to create urgency.

Email 2: The Value Adder

Sent 24 hours later

Subject line: "Still thinking about [product name]?" or "Your cart expires soon!"

Content: Provide additional information that helps the decision — size guides, styling tips, or customer reviews. Consider including a FAQ section addressing common purchase objections.

Email 3: The Final Push

Sent 48-72 hours later

Subject line: "Last chance! Your cart will be cleared soon" or "Special offer just for you!"

Content: This is where many businesses add an incentive — free shipping, a 10% discount, or a bonus gift with purchase. The key is making it feel exclusive, not desperate.

Advanced Personalization Tactics

Basic abandoned cart emails work, but personalization boosts results. Try these approaches:

- **Dynamic product recommendations**: "People who bought [abandoned item] also loved..."

- **Location-specific messaging**: "Get same-day delivery in [city]!"

- **Customer tier rewards**: "As a VIP member, you get free alterations!"

- **Time-sensitive bonuses**: "Complete within 6 hours for a free gift!"

Most ecommerce platforms (Shopify, WooCommerce) integrate directly with email tools to pull this data automatically.

Timing and Frequency Tweaks

While the standard sequence works for most, you can optimize further:

- **High-ticket items** ($500+): Space emails further apart (3-7 days)

- **Perishable goods**: Shorten the sequence to 24-36 hours total

- **B2B products**: Include a "Need a quote?" CTA alongside the cart recovery

Test different send times too — some audiences respond better to evening emails when they're relaxed, others to mid-morning messages.

Analyzing What Works

Your automation platform's analytics will show you:

- **Recovery rate**: What percentage of abandoned carts convert?

- **Email open/click patterns**: Which message resonates most?

- **Time-to-purchase**: How long after the email do people return?

- **Revenue impact**: Is the sequence driving meaningful sales?

Look for trends — maybe your second email performs best, suggesting you should move the incentive there. Or perhaps certain product categories have higher recovery rates, indicating where to focus.

Common Mistakes to Avoid

1. **Being too pushy**: "Why did you abandon your cart?" comes across as accusatory.

2. **Generic messaging**: "Complete your purchase" is less effective than referencing the specific items.

3. **Ignoring mobile users**: 60%+ of cart abandonment emails are opened on phones — design accordingly.

4. **Not testing subject lines**: Small changes can dramatically impact open rates.

5. **Forgetting post-purchase**: If they do buy, immediately stop the sequence!

Beyond Email: Multi-Channel Retargeting

For high-value carts, consider adding:

- **SMS reminders**: 3-5x higher open rates than email

- **Facebook/Instagram ads**: Retarget abandoners with the exact products

- **Browser push notifications**: "Your cart expires in 2 hours!"

These can be automated through most marketing platforms.

The Psychology Behind Effective Recovery

The most successful abandoned cart strategies tap into:

- **Loss aversion**: People hate missing out more than they love gaining

- **Social proof**: Showing others buying/approving the product

- **Scarcity**: Limited stock or time-bound offers

- **Authority**: Expert endorsements or media mentions

Your emails should subtly incorporate these principles without being manipulative.

Real-World Example

A boutique clothing store implemented this exact sequence:

1. Friendly reminder with product images (45% open rate)

2. Styling tips featuring the abandoned items (55% open rate)

3. Limited-time free shipping offer (60% open rate)

Result: 28% of abandoned carts recovered, adding $12,000/month in recovered revenue — all automated after the initial setup.

Getting Started with Your Own Sequence

Most email platforms have abandoned cart templates ready to customize. Start with:

1. Connect your ecommerce platform to your email tool

2. Set up the basic 3-email sequence

3. Add personalization where possible

4. Test different send times

5. Review analytics weekly at first

Remember — perfection isn't the goal. Just getting a basic sequence live will start recovering sales. You can always refine later.

The beauty of automation? Once set up, this system works 24/7, turning would-be lost sales into revenue while you focus on growing other parts of your business. Those abandoned carts aren't failures — they're opportunities waiting to be reclaimed.

Lesson 3: Organizing Lists and Analyzing Performance

Let me tell you about my friend Jake who runs an online fitness coaching business. He was sending the same weekly newsletter to all 5,000 subscribers and wondering why engagement kept dropping. Then he started segmenting his list - sending yoga content to yoga lovers and weightlifting tips to gym rats. Open rates jumped 45% in a month. That's the power of smart list organization and performance analysis we're about to dive into.

Why Blasting Everyone the Same Message Doesn't Work Anymore

Remember when email marketing meant uploading one giant list and hitting "send to all"? Those days are gone. Today's consumers expect content tailored to their interests and behaviors. A 22-year-old college athlete needs different messaging than a 55-year-old beginner. A loyal customer deserves different treatment than a first-time visitor.

Segmentation solves this by dividing your audience into smaller groups based on specific criteria. It's like hosting a dinner party - you wouldn't serve steak to vegetarians or talk retirement plans to college students. The same principle applies to your marketing.

Practical Ways to Segment Your Lists

Demographic Segmentation

- Age, gender, location, job title

- Best for: Local businesses, age-specific products
  Example: A skincare brand sends different anti-aging routines to 30-somethings vs 50-somethings

Behavioral Segmentation

- Purchase history, website activity, email engagement

- Best for: Ecommerce, content marketing
  Example: An online bookstore tags users who browse mystery novels differently from cookbook lovers

Customer Journey Stage

- New subscribers vs repeat buyers vs lapsed customers

- Best for: Nurture sequences, win-back campaigns
  Example: A SaaS company sends different onboarding emails to free trial users vs paying customers

Engagement Level

- Open/click rates, social media interactions

- Best for: Reactivation campaigns
  Example: A newsletter identifies "cold" subscribers who haven't opened in 90 days for a special re-engagement series

Psychographic Segmentation

- Values, interests, lifestyle

- Best for: Luxury brands, niche products
  Example: A sustainable fashion brand segments by customers who value eco-friendly materials vs those who prioritize style

Most email platforms let you create these segments using tags, custom fields, or smart lists that update automatically based on user actions.

Advanced Segmentation Strategies

Once you've mastered basic segments, try these powerful approaches:

Predictive Segmentation
Tools like ActiveCampaign can predict which subscribers are most likely to purchase based on past behavior, letting you focus efforts where they'll have most impact.

Lifecycle Marketing
Create segments based on customer milestones - 30 days since last purchase, annual renewal dates, or even birthdays.

Content Affinity
Tag subscribers based on which types of content they engage with most (videos, long-form articles, podcasts).

Combination Segments
Get really specific by combining multiple criteria, like "Women in California who bought yoga pants in the last 30 days but haven't opened emails in 2 weeks."

Tracking What Actually Matters

Open rates and click-through rates tell part of the story, but smart marketers track these more meaningful metrics:

Conversion Rate
What percentage of email recipients complete your desired action (purchase, signup, download)?

Revenue Per Email
Calculate how much money each campaign generates to identify your highest-performing content.

List Growth Rate
Are you adding subscribers faster than you're losing them?

Engagement Over Time
Identify when subscribers typically disengage to improve your nurture sequences.

Email Sharing/Forwarding
A strong indicator of truly valuable content.

Most email platforms provide these analytics, but the real magic happens when you connect your email data with Google Analytics to see the full customer journey.

Turning Data Into Action

Here's how to use your findings:

If certain segments have...

- **High open but low click rates**: Your subject lines work but content needs improvement

- **High clicks but low conversions**: Your landing page may need optimization

- **Quick unsubscribes**: You might be targeting the wrong audience or sending too frequently

Create a simple monthly review process:

1. Export key metrics to a spreadsheet

2. Identify 2-3 areas for improvement

3. Test one change per campaign

4. Compare results over time

Cleaning Your Lists

Segmentation only works if your lists stay fresh. Regular maintenance should include:

- Removing invalid email addresses (hard bounces)

- Flagging inactive subscribers for re-engagement campaigns

- Archiving unengaged contacts who don't respond to win-back attempts

- Updating customer records with new purchase/interaction data

Many tools can automate parts of this process, like automatically moving unengaged subscribers to a separate list after 6 months of inactivity.

Real-World Success Story

A home goods retailer segmented their list by:

1. Purchase history (kitchen vs bedroom buyers)

2. Geographic location (for seasonal promotions)

3. Engagement level (frequent vs occasional shoppers)

Result: 58% increase in email-driven revenue with 30% fewer sends, because every message became more relevant.

Getting Started With Your Own Segmentation

1. **Audit your current list**: What data do you already have?

2. **Pick 2-3 segmentation criteria** to start (don't overcomplicate)

3. **Create content tailored** to each segment's needs

4. **Track performance separately** for each group

5. **Refine monthly** based on what you learn

Remember - segmentation isn't about perfection. Even basic segmentation (like separating new subscribers from customers) will outperform bulk messaging. The more you practice, the better you'll understand your audience's unique needs and how to serve them.

When done right, segmentation and performance analysis transform your marketing from shouting into a crowd to having thoughtful one-on-one conversations at scale. And that's how you turn casual subscribers into loyal fans.

Your First Automated Email Campaign: A Step-by-Step Guide

Alright, time to roll up your sleeves — this is where theory meets practice. By the end of this task, you'll have a real, working email campaign that runs on autopilot. No coding or fancy skills needed — just follow these steps.

Step 1: Pick Your Tool

Choose one platform to start with (based on your business needs):

- **Mailchimp**: Best for beginners, especially if you're in ecommerce.

- **HubSpot**: Great if you want CRM + email combined.

- **ActiveCampaign**: Ideal for advanced automation (if you're ready to level up).

Not sure? Go with Mailchimp's free plan — it's the easiest for this exercise.

Step 2: Set Up Your Campaign Type

For this task, let's create a **welcome series** (the most useful starter campaign). Here's how:

1. **Log in** to your chosen tool.

2. Find the **Automation** or **Workflows** section (usually in the main menu).

3. Click **"Create Workflow"** and select **"Welcome Series"** (or "New Subscriber" if the option exists).

Step 3: Design Your First Email

Keep it simple. Your welcome email should:

- **Say thanks** ("Hey [First Name], thanks for joining us!")

- **Set expectations** ("You'll get weekly tips every Tuesday")

- **Offer value** (A discount, free guide, or your most popular content)

Pro tip: Use a friendly, conversational tone — like you're emailing a friend.

Step 4: Add a Trigger

This tells the system **when** to send the email. For a welcome series:

- Trigger = **"When someone subscribes"** (via your signup form).

Most tools auto-detect new subscribers — just confirm the trigger is set.

Step 5: Schedule the Next Emails (Optional but Powerful)

A single welcome email is good, but a **3-email sequence** works even better. Try this:

1. **Email 1**: Instant (Thanks + what to expect)

2. **Email 2**: 2 days later (Share your best content or product)

3. **Email 3**: 5 days later (Special offer or call-to-action)

Drag-and-drop the emails in your workflow builder to set the timing.

Step 6: Test Before Going Live

⚠ **Critical step!** Send test emails to yourself (and a colleague if possible). Check:

- Do links work?

- Does it look good on mobile?

- Is the tone right?

Fix any issues before activating.

Step 7: Turn It On!

Hit "**Activate**" or "**Start Workflow.**" Congrats — your campaign is now live!

What to Watch For

Over the next week, check:
✓ **Open rates** (Are people reading it?)
✓ **Click rates** (Are they engaging?)
✓ **Unsubscribes** (Is anything turning people off?)

Tweak as needed — maybe adjust the subject line or send time.

Final Tip: Start Small, Then Expand

Once this works, add:

- Abandoned cart emails (if you sell products)

- Birthday discounts (if you collect birthdates)

- Re-engagement emails (for inactive subscribers)

But for now? Just get **one** campaign running. Done is better than perfect!

Time needed: About 30-60 minutes (faster once you get the hang of it).

Need help? Google "[Your Tool] welcome email tutorial" — most have step-by-step videos.

Now go hit that "Activate" button — your future self (who's not manually sending emails) will thank you! 🚀

Unit 3: Social Media Automation

Let's be real—keeping up with social media feels like trying to drink from a firehose. Between posting consistently, replying to comments, and running ads, it's easy to get overwhelmed. But what if you could automate the repetitive parts while keeping that authentic human touch? That's exactly what we're diving into in this unit.

Social media automation isn't about becoming a robot. It's about working smarter so you can focus on what really matters—creating great content and building real connections. We'll walk through tools that help you schedule posts when your audience is actually online, set up quick replies for common questions, and even use chatbots to handle basic customer service.

You'll learn how to plan a week's worth of content in one sitting (instead of daily scrambling), set up rules to automatically engage with your audience, and track what's actually working so you can do more of that. The best part? Once you set these systems up, they keep working while you sleep, take weekends off, or focus on other parts of your business.

By the end, you'll have an automated social media campaign up and running—whether that's a scheduled content calendar, a chatbot for FAQs, or targeted ads that adjust themselves based on performance. We're making social media work for you, not the other way around.

Ready to take back your time while actually improving your social media results? Let's get started.

Lesson 1: Scheduling Posts and Automatic Engagement

Let me tell you about my friend Rachel who runs a small bakery. She used to post on Instagram randomly throughout her busy day - sometimes at 7am while prepping dough, other times at 10pm when she finally had a free moment. Her engagement was all over the place until she started scheduling posts in advance. Now she blocks out one hour every Sunday to plan her whole week's content, and her follower growth has doubled in three months. That's the power of smart social media scheduling we're going to explore.

Choosing Your Scheduling Sidekick

The right tool makes all the difference. Let's break down the top options:

Buffer is like the friendly neighborhood scheduling app - simple, intuitive, and perfect if you're just getting started. Their free plan lets you connect three social accounts and schedule up to 10 posts per channel. The clean interface means you'll be up and running in minutes. What I love about Buffer is how it suggests optimal posting times based on when your audience is most active.

Hootsuite is the Swiss Army knife of social tools - it can do everything from scheduling to analytics to team collaboration. Their free plan gives you 30 scheduled messages and lets you monitor multiple streams in one dashboard. Where Hootsuite really shines is for businesses that need to manage customer service across platforms - you can see all your mentions and messages in one place.

Later is the visual planner's dream, especially for Instagram. Their drag-and-drop calendar lets you see your entire content month at a glance. The free version includes 30 posts per month and their famous Linkin.bio feature that turns your Instagram profile into a clickable landing page.

Sprout Social offers more robust analytics and publishing features, making it great for growing businesses. While it doesn't have a free plan, the investment can be worth it if you're serious about scaling your social presence.

Finding Your Golden Posting Times

Here's the truth - there's no universal "best time to post." It depends entirely on your specific audience. But we can use some smart strategies to figure it out:

1. **Check Your Insights**

2. Every social platform provides analytics showing when your followers are online. On Instagram, go to your professional dashboard and look at "Audience Activity." Facebook shows similar data in Page Insights.

3. **Test Different Time Slots**

4. Try posting at various times for two weeks and track engagement. You might discover your foodie audience engages most at 7pm when they're thinking about dinner, while your B2B crowd is most active at 11am on weekdays.

5. **Consider Platform Nuances**

   - LinkedIn: Best Tuesday-Thursday, 8-10am or 12-2pm

- Twitter: Peak around lunchtime (12-1pm) and evenings (5-6pm)

- Instagram: Evenings and weekends often perform well

- Facebook: Midweek mid-morning through early afternoon

4. **Account for Time Zones**

If your audience is spread across regions, schedule some posts to hit multiple time zones. Many scheduling tools let you set specific times for different locations.

Smart Automation for Engagement

Automated responses get a bad rap when overused, but done right they can enhance your customer service. Here's how to use them effectively:

Comment Responses

Tools like ManyChat or Hootsuite's automated responses can handle frequently asked questions. For example:

- "Thanks for your comment! We'll get back to you soon."

- "Want to know when this product restocks? DM us 'Notify Me'!"

Direct Message Auto-Replies

Set up instant responses for common inquiries:

- Store hours

- Return policies

- Booking procedures

Engagement Rules

Platforms like Agorapulse let you create rules like:

- Automatically like comments containing certain keywords

- Send a follow-up DM to anyone who mentions a specific hashtag

- Flag posts with complaints for immediate human response

The key is balancing automation with human touch. Never automate sensitive topics - keep real people handling complaints, personal questions, and complex issues.

Creating Your Content Calendar

A solid scheduling strategy starts with planning. Here's a simple framework:

1. **Content Buckets**
   Divide your posts into categories like:

- Educational (tips, how-tos)

- Promotional (products, services)

- Engagement (polls, questions)

- Behind-the-scenes

2. **Posting Frequency**
   Start with:

- Instagram: 3-5x/week

- Facebook: 3-4x/week

- LinkedIn: 2-3x/week

- Twitter: 1-2x/day

3. **Batch Creation**
   Set aside 2-3 hours weekly to:

- Shoot multiple photos/videos

- Write captions

- Create graphics

4. **Scheduling**
   Use your chosen tool to:

- Upload posts

- Add captions and hashtags

- Set optimal times

- Preview how everything looks together

Pro Tips for Maximum Impact

- **Leave Room for Spontaneity**: Schedule 80% of your content, leaving 20% for timely posts

- **Repurpose Content**: Turn blog posts into Twitter threads, videos into Reels, etc.

- **Use Evergreen Content**: Create posts that stay relevant year-round for easy rescheduling

- **Monitor and Adjust**: Check analytics monthly to refine your strategy

Remember, scheduling isn't about being robotic - it's about creating consistency so you can focus on authentic engagement when it matters most. By taking the busywork out of social media, you free up time to actually connect with your audience in meaningful ways.

Now that you've got the blueprint, it's time to put it into action. In our next lesson, we'll dive into chatbots and more advanced automation. But first, master these fundamentals - they're the foundation of an effective social media strategy that works while you sleep.

Lesson 2: Using Bots in Social Network Management

Let me tell you about my friend Sarah who runs an online boutique. She was drowning in Instagram DMs - answering the same questions about sizing, shipping times, and return policies dozens of times a day. Then she implemented a simple chatbot. Now 60% of customer inquiries are handled automatically, her response time dropped from 12 hours to 12 minutes, and she got her evenings back. That's the power of smart bot automation we're going to explore.

Chatbots That Don't Feel Robotic

The key to effective social media bots is making them helpful, not annoying. Today's best chatbots can:

- Answer FAQs instantly (store hours, pricing, policies)

- Qualify leads before human handoff

- Process simple orders or bookings

- Collect customer feedback

- Route complex issues to the right team member

Facebook Messenger Bots
With over 1.3 billion users, Messenger is prime real estate for automated customer service. Tools like ManyChat and Chatfuel let you build no-code bots with:

- Quick reply buttons ("Track my order", "Start return")

- Menu-based navigation

- AI that understands variations of common questions

- Seamless transfer to live agents when needed

Instagram Automation
While Instagram's API restrictions are tighter, you can still:

- Set up quick replies for common DM questions

- Use "Saved Replies" for frequent comments

- Implement a Comment Guard bot to hide spam

- Create a "DM me" funnel in your bio link

The Human Touch Balance
Rule of thumb: Automate the predictable, humanize the emotional. Bots should handle:

- Order status requests

- Basic product questions

- Appointment scheduling

Humans should handle:

- Complaints

- Complex inquiries

- Personal styling advice

Campaign Management Bots

Beyond customer service, bots can supercharge your promotional efforts:

Lead Generation Bots
These engage users who interact with your ads or posts, collecting contact info and qualifying leads before your sales team gets involved. A simple flow might:

1. Ask if they want to receive special offers

2. Capture their email via Facebook's native form

3. Send an immediate discount code

4. Tag them in your CRM for follow-up

Quiz Bots

Interactive quizzes ("Find your perfect skincare routine") are incredibly effective for both engagement and data collection. Tools like Typeform integrate with chat platforms to:

- Educate customers about your products

- Recommend personalized solutions

- Build detailed customer profiles

Giveaway & Contest Bots

Automate the entire entry process:

- Accept submissions via comments/DMs

- Verify entries (follow, tag friends, etc.)

- Select and notify winners

- Deliver prizes

Choosing Your Bot Platform

For Beginners

- ManyChat: Intuitive visual builder, great for ecommerce

- MobileMonkey: Omnichannel support across platforms

For Advanced Users

- Dialogflow: Google's AI-powered natural language processing

- IBM Watson: Enterprise-grade conversation intelligence

All-in-One Solutions

- HubSpot Conversations: Combines bots with full CRM

- Zendesk Answer Bot: Integrates with existing help desk

Implementation Best Practices

1. **Start Small**
   Begin with 3-5 most common questions before expanding

2. **Keep It Conversational**
   Write bot scripts like a friendly assistant, not a robot

3. **Set Clear Handoff Points**
   When the bot gets stuck, ensure smooth transfer to humans

4. **Analyze & Optimize**
   Review transcripts monthly to find where bots fail or succeed

5. **Promote Your Bot**
   Use Facebook's "Send Message" CTAs and Instagram's "Get Started" button

Real-World Success Story

A local spa implemented a booking bot that:

- Answers questions about services

- Shows real-time availability

- Takes deposits via Messenger payments

Result: 40% of bookings now happen after hours, with 90% customer satisfaction on bot interactions.

Avoiding Bot Pitfalls

- Don't over-automate - some conversations need human nuance

- Always include "Talk to a person" options

- Regularly update your bot's knowledge base

- Never use bots for sensitive topics (medical, legal, etc.)

The Future of Social Bots

Emerging trends include:

- Voice-enabled assistants for social platforms

- AI that learns from every conversation

- Bots that proactively message based on user behavior

- Integration with AR for virtual try-ons via chat

Remember: The goal isn't to replace human connection, but to enhance it by automating the repetitive so you can focus on the meaningful. When implemented thoughtfully, social media bots become like helpful team members that work 24/7 to grow your business while you sleep.

In our next lesson, we'll explore how to track and optimize all these automated efforts. But first, try setting up one simple bot flow - you'll be amazed at the time it saves.

Lesson 3: Analyzing Social Media Campaign Performance

Let me share a story about my client, a small coffee roastery. They were posting beautiful photos daily but couldn't understand why some got 500+ likes while others barely cracked 50. After digging into their analytics, we discovered their audience engaged most with behind-the-scenes roasting videos - something they'd only posted occasionally. By shifting their content mix based on these insights, they doubled their engagement rate in six weeks. That's the power of data-driven social media management we're about to explore.

Moving Beyond Vanity Metrics

Likes and follows feel good, but they don't pay the bills. The metrics that actually matter fall into three categories:

Engagement Metrics

- **Engagement Rate**: (Likes + Comments + Shares)/Followers × 100

- **Click-Through Rate**: Link clicks ÷ Impressions

- **Saved Posts**: Indicates highly valuable content

- **Story Completion Rates**: Who watches your stories all the way through?

Conversion Metrics

- Website visits from social

- Lead form completions

- Promo code usage

- Direct purchases attributed to social

Audience Growth Metrics

- Follower growth rate

- Quality of new followers (do they engage?)

- Best-performing acquisition sources

Platform-Specific Insights

Each social network provides unique analytics worth monitoring:

Instagram Insights

- Reach vs. Impressions (are you reaching new people?)

- Profile visits (are people exploring after seeing your post?)

- Top performing hashtags

Facebook Analytics

- Negative feedback (hides/unfollows)

- Peak engagement times by day

- Video retention rates

LinkedIn Metrics

- Demographic breakdown of your audience

- Content sharing patterns

- Follower job function/industry

Twitter Analytics

- Best-performing tweet types (threads, polls, media)

- Link click patterns

- Follower interests

Making Data Actionable

Raw numbers are useless without interpretation. Here's how to extract insights:

1. **Spot Patterns**
   Look for commonalities in your top-performing posts:

- Specific content formats (videos, carousels, etc.)

- Posting times/days

- Hashtag combinations

- Caption styles

2. **Identify Underperformers**
   Analyze flops to understand what to avoid:

- Was the timing off?

- Did the visual underdeliver?

- Was the call-to-action unclear?

3. **Benchmark Against Goals**
   Compare results to your original KPIs:

- Did you aim for comments but get mostly likes?

- Wanted link clicks but got saves instead?

- Expected shares but saw minimal?

Optimization Strategies

Based on your findings, you might:

- **Adjust Posting Frequency**: More/less often

- **Shift Content Mix**: Double down on what works

- **Experiment with Formats**: Try Reels if static posts underperform

- **Refine Targeting**: Adjust audience parameters

- **Optimize Posting Times**: Align with peak engagement

Tools to Automate Analysis

Platforms like Sprout Social, Hootsuite Analytics, and Google Data Studio can:

- Generate automatic performance reports

- Highlight statistically significant changes

- Predict optimal posting times

- Benchmark against competitors

Creating a Continuous Improvement Cycle

1. **Test**: Try one variable at a time (caption style, image type, etc.)

2. **Measure**: Track performance against control posts

3. **Learn**: Identify what moved the needle

4. **Implement**: Apply successful elements broadly

5. **Repeat**: Ongoing refinement beats occasional overhauls

Common Pitfalls to Avoid

- **Analysis Paralysis**: Don't get stuck in spreadsheets - act on insights

- **Over-Indexing on One Metric**: Balance engagement with conversions

- **Ignoring Qualitative Data**: Read comments for context behind numbers

- **Chasing Algorithm Changes**: Focus on audience needs over platform whims

Real-World Optimization Example

A boutique hotel chain noticed through analytics that:

- Room tour videos outperformed photo carousels by 300%

- Posts tagging local attractions drove more saves

- Weekend evening posts got more engagement

They adjusted their strategy to:

- Produce two video tours weekly

- Partner with nearby restaurants for co-tagged content

- Schedule prime posts for Saturday evenings

Result: 40% increase in direct bookings from Instagram within a quarter.

Building Your Analytics Routine

1. **Weekly Check-Ins**

- Review top/underperforming posts

- Note any significant changes

2. **Monthly Deep Dives**

- Analyze trends over time

- Adjust strategy as needed

3. **Quarterly Audits**

- Evaluate overall progress toward goals

- Refresh content pillars based on data

Remember: Analytics shouldn't stifle creativity - they should inform it. The numbers tell you what's working so you can do more of it, not so you can turn into a content robot. Keep testing, keep learning, and let the data guide - not dictate - your social media strategy.

Hands-On: Create Your First Automated Social Media Campaign

Let's cut to the chase—you've learned the theory, now it's time to actually **build** something. By the end of this task, you'll have a real, working social media automation sequence running on autopilot. No fluff, just a step-by-step guide to get results.

Step 1: Pick Your Tool & Platform

Choose **one** combo to start (don't overthink it):

- **For beginners**: Buffer + Instagram

- **For customer service**: ManyChat + Facebook Messenger

- **For content-heavy brands**: Hootsuite + Twitter/LinkedIn

Stuck? Go with **Buffer**—it's the easiest for scheduling posts.

Step 2: Define Your Goal

What's this campaign for? Pick **one** focus:

- **Growth**: Attract new followers

- **Engagement**: Boost comments/shares

- **Sales**: Drive traffic to your website

- **Service**: Automate FAQs

Example: A bakery might automate a "Weekly Featured Dessert" post to boost orders.

Step 3: Set Up the Automation

Option A: Scheduling Posts (e.g., Buffer/Hootsuite)

1. **Connect your social account** to the tool.

2. **Create a content calendar** for the next 7 days (3-5 posts).

3. **Write captions** (use emojis, questions, or CTAs).

4. **Upload media** (images/videos).

5. **Schedule times** (use the tool's "best time" suggestions).

6. **Add hashtags** (5-10 relevant ones).

Pro tip: Mix post types—1 educational, 1 promotional, 1 fun/behind-the-scenes.

Option B: Chatbot Replies (e.g., ManyChat)

1. **Set up triggers**:

   o Keywords ("price," "hours," "track order")

   o Instagram DM quick replies

   o Facebook comments ("DM 'MENU' for deals")

2. **Write responses**:

   o Friendly, concise answers

   o Buttons for options ("1. Pricing | 2. Support")

3. **Add a human handoff**:

   o "Need more help? Reply 'AGENT' to chat live!"

Pro tip: Test with a colleague first — does the bot sound natural?

Step 4: Add Engagement Rules

Most tools let you automate:

- **Liking/following** posts with your hashtags

- **Thanking new followers** (avoid spammy DMs — just a quick "Thanks!")

- **Replying to comments** (e.g., "Thanks! 😊 Want the recipe? DM me!")

Keep it light — automation should feel human, not robotic.

Step 5: Test & Launch

- **Dry run**: Schedule 1-2 test posts to check formatting.

- **Review**: Do links work? Do replies sound natural?

- **Go live**: Hit "Start Campaign" and let it run.

Step 6: Track & Tweak

After 3-7 days, check:
✓ **Engagement rate** (likes/comments per follower)
✓ **Click-throughs** (if linking to a website)
✓ **Follower growth** (for growth campaigns)

Adjust: Double down on what works, ditch what flops.

Real-World Example

A fitness coach used **Hootsuite** to:

1. Schedule daily workout tips at 7 AM (when her audience was most active).

2. Auto-reply to "How do I start?" DMs with a free guide link.

3. Like posts with her branded hashtag to boost community engagement.

Result: 40% more leads in a month, with 5 hours/week saved.

Final Tips

- **Start small**: Automate just 1 thing (e.g., post scheduling OR chatbot replies).

- **Stay human**: Use casual language ("Hey there!" vs. "Dear valued customer").

- **Optimize weekly**: Tweak timings, captions, or responses based on data.

Time needed: 30-60 mins (faster once you're familiar).

Done? Congrats! You've just freed up hours each week. Now go enjoy that extra time — you've earned it. 🚀

P.S. Hit a snag? Google "[Your Tool] + [Issue]" — there's always a tutorial or forum post to help.

Unit 4: Paid Advertising Automation

Let's talk about something that used to drive me crazy - constantly tweaking ad campaigns, checking performance every few hours, and still feeling like I was leaving money on the table. Then I discovered advertising automation, and it completely changed the game.

Paid ads don't have to be a full-time job. With the right automation strategies, your campaigns can practically run themselves while you sleep, automatically adjusting bids, finding better audiences, and pausing underperformers - all while you focus on other parts of your business.

In this unit, we're going to cut through the complexity and show you exactly how to set up self-optimizing ad campaigns that actually work. Whether you're using Google Ads, Facebook, or another platform, the principles are the same: let the algorithms do what they're good at (crunching numbers) while you focus on what you're good at (growing your business).

We'll start with the basics of automated bidding - no more guessing what to bid or wasting money on clicks that don't convert. Then we'll dive into how AI can help you find your perfect customers, even ones you didn't know existed. Finally, we'll make sure you're tracking the right metrics so your campaigns keep getting better over time.

By the end, you'll be running ads that adjust themselves in real-time based on performance, target high-value customers automatically, and give you clear reports showing exactly where your money's going. No more throwing darts in the dark - just consistent, scalable results.

Ready to stop babysitting your ads and start scaling them? Let's dive in.

Lesson 1: Automating Paid Ad Campaigns (PPC)

Let me tell you about my friend Sarah who runs an e-commerce store selling handmade candles. She was spending hours every day manually adjusting her Google Ads bids - raising them when sales were slow, lowering them when conversions dropped. It was exhausting. Then she discovered automated bidding strategies. Within a month, her cost per acquisition dropped by 30% while her conversion rate increased. She got her evenings back while her ads worked smarter, not harder. That's exactly what we're going to help you achieve.

Why Manual Bidding is Like Driving With Your Eyes Closed

Remember when PPC meant setting fixed bids and checking them constantly? Those days are gone. Today's automated bidding is like having a co-pilot who knows every turn in the road before you get there. Here's why it works:

1. **Machines Process Data Faster**: Google's algorithms can evaluate millions of signals in milliseconds - things like device type, location, time of day, and even weather conditions that might affect buyer behavior.

2. **Real-Time Adjustments**: Automated systems respond instantly to changes in competition or conversion rates, something no human can do 24/7.

3. **Goal-Oriented Optimization**: Instead of guessing at bids, you tell the system exactly what you want (more conversions, lower costs, etc.) and it figures out how to get there.

Google Ads Automation: Your New Best Friend

Google offers several smart bidding strategies, each designed for specific goals:

For Maximum Conversions

- Best for: Businesses focused on getting as many conversions as possible within their budget

- How it works: Automatically sets bids to get the most conversions while spending your entire budget

- Pro tip: Use when you have at least 30 conversions in the past 30 days

For Target CPA (Cost Per Acquisition)

- Best for: Businesses with a specific cost-per-customer goal

- How it works: Sets bids to get as many conversions as possible at your target cost

- Real-world example: If you know you can afford $20 per new customer, set this as your target

For Target ROAS (Return On Ad Spend)

- Best for: E-commerce stores with varying product values

- How it works: Optimizes bids to hit your desired return on investment

- Sweet spot: Works best when you have conversion value tracking set up

Enhanced CPC

- Best for: Those who want a hybrid approach

- How it works: Adjusts your manual bids up or down based on conversion likelihood

- When to use: Good for testing the waters before going all-in on automation

Setting Up Your First Automated Campaign

Let's walk through creating a Target CPA campaign:

1. **Navigate to your Google Ads account** and click "Campaigns"

2. **Click the blue "+" button** to create a new campaign

3. **Select your campaign goal** (Sales, Leads, etc.)

4. **Choose your campaign type** (Search, Display, etc.)

5. **Set your budget and bidding strategy** - this is where you'll select "Target CPA"

6. **Enter your target CPA** based on historical data

7. **Complete setting up** your ad groups, keywords, and ads as usual

The magic happens after you launch. Google's machine learning will:

- Analyze which searches lead to conversions

- Adjust bids in real-time based on conversion likelihood

- Shift budget toward better-performing keywords

- Learn and improve over time (usually takes about 2 weeks)

Common Pitfalls (And How to Avoid Them)

1. **Not Enough Conversion Data**

   o Fix: Wait until you have at least 30 conversions before using smart bidding

2. **Setting Unrealistic Targets**

   o Fix: Base your CPA/ROAS goals on historical performance, not wishful thinking

3. **Frequent Strategy Changes**

   o Fix: Stick with a strategy for at least 2-3 weeks before evaluating

4. **Poor Conversion Tracking**

   o Fix: Double-check your Google Ads conversion tracking is working properly

Advanced Automation Features

Once you're comfortable with basic automated bidding, explore:

Seasonal Adjustments
Tell Google about upcoming sales or holidays so it can anticipate demand changes

Portfolio Bid Strategies
Manage multiple campaigns with a single strategy and budget

Target Impression Share
Great for brand awareness campaigns where visibility is key

Real-World Success Story

A local HVAC company switched from manual bidding to Target CPA automation. Results after 60 days:

- 42% increase in conversions

- 27% lower cost per lead

- 15 hours per week saved on bid management
  All while handling 35% more inbound calls during peak season.

Your Action Plan

1. **Audit your current campaigns** - identify which could benefit most from automation

2. **Start with one campaign** - don't automate everything at once

3. **Choose the right strategy** based on your primary goal

4. **Set realistic targets** using your historical data

5. **Monitor but don't micromanage** - give the algorithm time to learn

6. **Tweak after 2-3 weeks** based on performance

Remember, automation isn't "set it and forget it" - it's "set it up right, then let it work while you focus elsewhere." The machines handle the number-crunching so you can focus on strategy and growth.

In our next lesson, we'll dive into how AI can take your targeting to the next level. But first, try automating one campaign - you might be surprised how quickly it outperforms your manual efforts.

Lesson 2: Optimizing Campaigns with Artificial Intelligence

Remember when targeting ads meant guessing demographics and hoping for the best? Those days are gone. Today's AI-powered tools can analyze thousands of data points to find your perfect customers - even ones you never knew existed. Let me show you how to leverage this technology without needing a degree in data science.

How AI Actually Works in Advertising

The magic happens through machine learning algorithms that continuously analyze:

- Who engages with your ads

- What actions they take afterward

- Patterns in successful conversions

- Real-time shifts in audience behavior

Unlike traditional targeting that relies on static demographics, AI adapts daily. It might discover your product appeals to:

- Empty nesters rather than young parents

- Night owls rather than early birds

- Android users over iPhone owners

These are insights you'd likely never uncover manually.

Facebook's AI Optimization Tools

Advantage+ Audience
This feature is like having a supercharged marketing assistant. Instead of guessing interests, you:

1. Define your conversion goal (purchases, leads, etc.)

2. Provide a broad audience (age/location only)

3. Let Facebook's AI find the right people

Case Study: A pet food brand used this and discovered their best customers were actually urban singles in their 30s, not suburban families as they'd assumed.

Automatic Placements
Allows Facebook to distribute your ads across:

- Feed

- Stories

- Reels

- Marketplace

- Audience Network

The AI determines where each user is most likely to engage.

Dynamic Creative
Upload multiple:

- Images/videos

- Headlines

- Descriptions

- CTAs

Facebook then mixes and matches to show the best combo to each user.

Google's Smart Campaigns

For smaller businesses, Google's AI-powered Smart Campaigns:

- Automatically create ads from your website content

- Adjust bids in real-time

- Optimize for calls or website visits

- Require just 15 minutes to set up

Perfect for:

- Local service businesses

- E-commerce stores

- Appointment-based services

Advanced AI Tools Worth Exploring

AdCreative.ai
Generates high-converting ad creatives by analyzing what works in your industry.

Pattern89
Predicts ad performance before you launch using historical data.

Pinterest Predict

Identifies emerging trends before they peak.

Implementing AI Without Losing the Human Touch

1. **Start with clear conversion tracking**
   AI needs clean data - ensure your pixels and tags are properly installed.

2. **Feed the algorithm quality inputs**
   Upload customer lists, catalog items, and creative assets.

3. **Set guardrails**
   Establish:

- Budget limits

- Brand safety parameters

- Negative audiences

4. **Review and refine weekly**
   AI improves with human oversight - check what it's discovering.

Real-World Results

A boutique saw 3X ROAS after implementing AI optimizations:

1. Used Advantage+ Audience

2. Enabled dynamic creative

3. Let AI handle placements

4. Maintained brand voice in ads

Your Action Plan

1. **Test one AI feature** per campaign (start with Advantage+ or Smart Bidding)

2. **Give it 2-3 weeks** to learn before evaluating

3. **Compare performance** against your manual campaigns

4. **Scale what works** and iterate

Remember: AI works best when combined with your market knowledge. The technology handles the "who" and "when," while you control the "what" and "why" of your messaging.

Next, we'll explore how to measure all these automated efforts - because what gets measured gets improved. But first, try implementing one AI optimization in your current campaigns. You might be surprised by who your real best customers turn out to be.

Lesson 3: Measuring and Analyzing Automated Ad Results

Let me tell you about my client, a local bakery that was spending $2,000/month on Facebook ads with mixed results. They couldn't figure out why some weeks brought floods of customers while others were complete duds. Then we dug into their ad analytics and discovered something surprising - their weekend afternoon ads were getting tons of engagement but almost no conversions, while their weekday morning ads (which looked identical) were driving most of their sales. This one insight helped them reallocate their budget and increase revenue by 40% without spending an extra dime. That's the power of proper ad analysis we're going to explore today.

Cutting Through the Data Noise

When you first look at ad metrics, it's easy to get overwhelmed. Here's how to focus on what actually matters:

For Brand Awareness:

- Reach and frequency

- Video completion rates

- Brand lift studies

For Engagement:

- Comments and shares

- Time spent viewing

- Click-through rate (CTR)

For Conversions:

- Cost per acquisition (CPA)

- Return on ad spend (ROAS)

- Conversion rate

For Retention:

- Repeat customer rate

- Customer lifetime value (LTV)

- Retention cost

Setting Up Proper Tracking

Before you can analyze anything, you need clean data:

1. **Install the Facebook Pixel** or Google Tag Manager

2. **Set up conversion events** (purchases, signups, etc.)

3. **Implement UTM parameters** for campaign tracking

4. **Connect to Google Analytics** for full-funnel visibility

Pro tip: Test your tracking by completing test conversions to ensure everything's recording properly.

Reading Automated Reports

Most platforms now offer AI-powered insights. Here's how to interpret them:

Facebook's Automated Rules
Can automatically:

- Pause underperforming ads

- Increase budget for winning ads

- Notify you of significant changes

Google's Recommendations
Suggestions like:

- "Bid higher on these keywords"

- "Remove these low-performing placements"

- "Try these new audience segments"

Third-Party Tools
Platforms like Hyros or TripleWhale provide:

- Cross-channel attribution

- Profit-based optimization

- Creative performance breakdowns

Making Data-Driven Adjustments

When you spot an underperforming ad:

1. **Check the creative** - Is the image/video still relevant?

2. **Review the audience** - Has it become saturated?

3. **Analyze the offer** - Is the CTA still compelling?

4. **Consider external factors** - Seasonality, competition, etc.

For winning ads:

1. **Scale horizontally** - Test similar creatives

2. **Scale vertically** - Increase budget gradually

3. **Expand audiences** - Lookalikes, broader interests

Creating Your Optimization Routine

Daily:

- Check for technical issues (broken links, disapproved ads)

- Review automated rule actions

Weekly:

- Analyze winning/underperforming assets

- Adjust budgets based on performance

- Test 1-2 new variables

Monthly:

- Review customer acquisition cost trends

- Calculate overall ROAS

- Plan bigger tests and strategy shifts

Real-World Optimization Example

An e-commerce store noticed:

- 4% CTR but only 0.5% conversion rate

- High cart abandonment after shipping page

They:

1. Added free shipping threshold messaging to ads

2. Created a retargeting campaign for abandoners

3. Optimized their checkout flow

Result: 3X more conversions at same ad spend.

Key Metrics Benchmarks

While every industry differs, here are healthy starting points:

- Facebook/Instagram:

  o CTR: 1-2%

  o CPC: 0.50−0.50−1.50

  o ROAS: 3-4X

- Google Ads:

  o CTR: 2-3% (Search), 0.5-1% (Display)

  o Conversion rate: 3-5%

  o CPA: Varies widely by industry

Avoiding Analysis Paralysis

Remember:

- Not every fluctuation requires action

- Look at trends, not single data points

- Sometimes the best optimization is no optimization

Your Action Plan

1. **Set up proper tracking** if you haven't already

2. **Export last month's data** into a simple spreadsheet

3. **Identify your best/worst performers**

4. **Make one strategic change** based on insights

5. **Document results** to inform future tests

The most successful advertisers aren't those who check stats obsessively, but those who build systems to automatically surface insights and take calculated actions. That's the balance we're aiming for - leveraging automation's power while maintaining human oversight.

In our next unit, we'll explore how to automate your reporting so you spend less time compiling data and more time acting on it. But first, try analyzing one campaign with these principles - you'll likely spot opportunities you've been missing.

Hands-On: Launch Your First Automated Ad Campaign

Let's cut through the theory and get your hands dirty. By the end of this task, you'll have a real, automated ad campaign running — whether on **Google Ads** or **Facebook/Instagram** — using smart optimization techniques to maximize results.

Step 1: Choose Your Platform & Goal

Pick **one** platform and objective to start:

Option A: Google Ads (Best for Search & Direct Conversions)

- **Campaign Type**: Search, Display, or Shopping

- **Goal**: Website visits, calls, or purchases

- **Automation Focus**: Smart Bidding (Target CPA or ROAS)

Option B: Facebook/Instagram (Best for Engagement & Brand Awareness)

- **Campaign Type**: Traffic, Conversions, or Catalog Sales

- **Goal**: Lead gen, online sales, or app installs

- **Automation Focus**: Advantage+ Audience & Dynamic Creative

Step 2: Set Up Your Campaign with Automation

For Google Ads (Smart Bidding)

1. **Create a new campaign** → Select your goal (Sales, Leads, etc.).

2. **Choose "Automated bidding"** → Pick **Target CPA** (if you know your cost-per-acquisition) or **Maximize Conversions** (if you're just starting).

3. **Set a realistic CPA** (check past data or industry benchmarks).

4. **Add your keywords/audiences** (keep them broad — let Google's AI optimize).

5. **Enable "Smart Display" or "Dynamic Search Ads"** (if running Display/Search).

6. **Launch and monitor** (but don't tweak for at least 3-5 days).

For Facebook/Instagram (AI Optimization)

1. **Go to Ads Manager** → Create a **Conversions** or **Traffic** campaign.

2. **Toggle on "Advantage+ Audience"** (lets Facebook find the best people).

3. **Use "Dynamic Creative"** → Upload 3-5 images/videos + multiple ad copies.

4. **Set up Automated Rules** (e.g., "Pause ads with CPA > $X").

5. **Launch and review** after 48 hours.

Step 3: Apply at Least One Automation Technique

Pick **one** advanced tactic to test:

☑ **Google Ads:**

- **Seasonal Adjustments** (if running holiday promotions)

- **Portfolio Bid Strategy** (manage multiple campaigns under one automated rule)

☑ **Facebook/Instagram:**

- **Automatic Placements** (let Meta choose where your ads perform best)

- **CBO (Campaign Budget Optimization)** (automatically allocates budget to top-performing ads)

Step 4: Track & Optimize (Without Micromanaging)

After 3-7 days, check:

📊 **Key Metrics:**

- **Google:** CTR, Conversion Rate, CPA

- **Facebook:** ROAS, Cost per Lead, Engagement Rate

✘ **Quick Optimizations:**

- **Scale up** what's working (increase budget by 20-30% for winning ads).

- **Pause** underperformers (ads with high spend but low conversions).

- **Test** one new variable (e.g., a different headline or audience).

Real-World Example

A fitness coach used **Facebook Advantage+ Audience + Dynamic Creative** to:

- Reduce cost per lead from 8to8to4.

- Automatically shift budget to Reels ads (which outperformed Stories).

- Save 5+ hours/week on manual adjustments.

Final Tips

◆ **Don't over-optimize early** — AI needs time to learn (wait 3-5 days before changes).

◆ **Start small** — test one automation feature before adding more.

◆ **Use rules** — automate bid adjustments and budget reallocation.

Time needed: ~45 minutes to set up, then 10 mins/day to monitor.

Done? Congrats! You've just launched a self-optimizing ad campaign. 🚀

Next step: Check back in 3 days to review performance and make light tweaks.

(Need help? Google "[Your Platform] + [Automation Technique] tutorial" — there's always a step-by-step guide!)

Unit 5: Automating Data Analysis and Reporting

Let's be honest—most marketers hate reporting. You spend hours pulling numbers from different platforms, wrestling with spreadsheets, and creating slides that nobody reads. But what if your reports could build themselves while you sleep? What if you could spot trends before they become problems and opportunities before your competitors do? That's exactly what we're going to make happen in this unit.

Data is only powerful when it's actionable. Right now, you're probably sitting on a goldmine of insights trapped in different tools—Google Analytics, your CRM, social platforms, ad accounts. We're going to connect these silos and turn that raw data into clear, automatic reports that actually help you make decisions.

You'll learn how to set up dashboards that update in real-time, create alerts for when important metrics change, and build systems that learn from your data to suggest improvements. The best part? Once you set this up, it keeps working—no more last-minute report scrambling before meetings.

By the end of this unit, you'll have a living, breathing reporting system that doesn't just tell you what happened, but helps you decide what to do next. Whether you need to impress your boss, guide your team, or just understand what's actually working in your marketing, we'll build the tools to make it effortless.

Ready to stop drowning in data and start riding the waves of insight? Let's dive in.

Lesson 1: Integrating Analytics Tools

You know that feeling when you're trying to understand your marketing performance but have twelve different tabs open - Google Analytics, Facebook Ads, your email platform, maybe a CRM? And none of them talk to each other? That's what we're going to fix today.

Why Connecting Your Tools Changes Everything

Imagine this instead: One dashboard that shows you exactly how your Facebook ads are impacting email signups, which blog posts are actually driving sales, and where your marketing funnel has leaks. That's the power of connecting your analytics tools.

Here's what happens when you break down those data silos:

- You stop guessing which campaigns are working

- Your reports actually make sense to non-marketers

- You can track a customer's entire journey

- Decisions get easier because you're looking at the full picture

Google Analytics: Your Marketing Truth-Teller

Most people use GA like a simple traffic counter. Big mistake. Here's how the pros use it:

Setting Up Proper Tracking

- Install the global site tag (gtag.js) properly

- Configure goals for key actions (purchases, signups, etc.)

- Set up enhanced ecommerce tracking if you sell products

- Link to Google Ads and Search Console

The Reports You're Probably Missing

- **Behavior Flow**: See where people drop off

- **Multi-Channel Funnels**: How touchpoints work together

- **Custom Segments**: Compare mobile vs desktop, new vs returning

Pro Tip: Create a custom dashboard with just the 5-7 metrics that actually matter to your business.

Power BI: Where the Magic Happens

While Google Analytics shows website data, Power BI connects everything:

- Website analytics

- Ad platforms (Facebook, Google, etc.)

- Email marketing stats

- CRM/sales data

- Social media metrics

Getting Started

1. Download Power BI Desktop (free)

2. Connect your data sources

3. Build relationships between datasets

4. Create visualizations that tell stories

Game-Changer Feature: Power BI's AI insights can automatically spot trends and anomalies you'd miss.

Connecting The Dots

Here's how to make your tools talk to each other:

Google Analytics + Google Ads

- Link the accounts in GA admin settings

- Import GA goals into Google Ads as conversions

- View GA data directly in Google Ads reports

Facebook Pixel + Google Analytics

- Set up cross-domain tracking

- Create UTM parameters for Facebook traffic

- Compare Facebook stats in both platforms

CRM + Everything Else

- Use Zapier to push lead data from forms to your CRM

- Set up custom dimensions in GA for CRM data

- Create Power BI dashboards that blend all sources

Real-World Example

An online course company connected:

- Their Teachable platform (sales)

- Facebook/Google Ads

- Email marketing (ActiveCampaign)

- Google Analytics

The result? They discovered:

- Their "free webinar" converted better than direct sales

- Email follow-ups drove 32% of all sales

- Certain ad audiences had higher lifetime value

This let them:

- Increase ad spend on high-LTV groups

- Automate email sequences for webinar no-shows

- Reduce wasted spend on poor-converting traffic

Common Integration Mistakes

1. **Not filtering internal traffic** - skews all your data

2. **Mismatched attribution models** - last click vs first click

3. **Forgetting mobile tracking** - huge blind spot

4. **Not setting up conversion values** - can't calculate ROAS

Your Action Plan

1. **Audit your current setup** - what tools aren't connected?

2. **Pick one integration** to implement this week (start with GA + your ads)

3. **Build one custom report** that combines data sources

4. **Schedule monthly check-ins** to refine your tracking

Remember: You don't need perfect data to start - just better data than you have now. Every connection you make gives you sharper insights and smarter decisions.

In our next lesson, we'll automate these reports so they land in your inbox ready to use. But first, try connecting just two of your tools - that first "aha" moment when the data clicks is priceless.

Pro tip: If you get stuck, most platforms have step-by-step integration guides - just search "[Tool A] connect to [Tool B]" and you'll find instructions.

Lesson 2: Setting Up Automated Reports

Let me tell you about my friend Alex who runs an e-commerce store. Every Monday morning, he'd spend 3-4 hours pulling numbers from Google Analytics, Facebook Ads, and his email platform to create a weekly performance report for his team. Then he discovered automated reporting. Now, that same report lands in his inbox (and his team's) every Monday at 7 AM sharp, without him lifting a finger. Even better - it's actually more accurate and useful than his manual versions ever were.

Why Automated Reporting is a Game-Changer

Think about what happens when reports are manual:

- You waste hours compiling data instead of analyzing it

- Human errors creep in (wrong filters, missed date ranges)

- By the time you finish, the data is already outdated

- Different team members look at different numbers

Automated reporting fixes all this by:
✓ Delivering fresh data on schedule
✓ Eliminating spreadsheet errors
✓ Giving everyone the same numbers to work from
✓ Freeing you up to actually use the insights

Choosing What to Automate First

Not all reports deserve automation. Start with these high-impact candidates:

1. The Daily Pulse Check

- Key metrics that need constant monitoring

- Example: Website conversions, ad spend, inventory levels

- Best for: Quick morning reviews

2. The Weekly Performance Digest

- Campaign-level results

- Week-over-week comparisons

- Best for: Team meetings and strategy adjustments

3. The Monthly Deep Dive

- Full-funnel analysis

- ROI calculations

- Best for: Executive reviews and planning

Tools That Make It Easy

Google Data Studio (Now Looker Studio)

- Free tool from Google

- Connects to 500+ data sources

- Customizable dashboards

- Schedule email deliveries

Power BI

- More advanced analytics

- Handles larger datasets

- Better for combining multiple sources

Platform-Specific Options

- Facebook Ads Manager scheduled reports

- Google Analytics email summaries

- CRM export automations

Building Your First Automated Report

Let's create a weekly marketing performance report in Google Data Studio:

1. **Connect Your Data Sources**

- Google Analytics

- Google Ads

- Facebook Ads (via connector)

2. **Design the Layout**

- Header: Date range, summary metrics

- Section 1: Traffic sources

- Section 2: Campaign performance

- Section 3: Conversion funnels

3. **Add Smart Visualizations**

- Scorecards for key metrics

- Time series graphs for trends

- Tables for detailed data

4. **Set Up Scheduling**

- Choose "Schedule email delivery"

- Set to every Monday at 7 AM

- Add recipient emails

5. **Add Commentary**
   Use the "Notes" feature to:

- Highlight big changes

- Call out areas needing attention

- Suggest next steps

Making Reports Actually Useful

The best reports:
◆ Fit on one page (or one screen)
◆ Start with key takeaways
◆ Use color coding for good/bad results
◆ Compare to goals and past periods
◆ Link to underlying data for drill-down

Avoid "data puking" - where you dump every metric possible without focus.

Real-World Example

An agency automated their client reports with:

- 1-page executive summary

- 3 key metrics front and center

- Automated commentary based on results

- Scheduled delivery 2 hours before check-in calls

Result: Prep time dropped from 3 hours to 15 minutes per client, while client satisfaction scores improved because the reports were clearer and more consistent.

Taking It Further

Once you're comfortable, try:

- ☑ Alert-based reporting (get notified when metrics hit thresholds)
- ☑ Team-specific versions (sales gets different data than marketing)
- ☑ Automated slide decks (for board meetings)
- ☑ Voice-activated analytics (ask Alexa for your numbers)

Common Pitfalls

1. **Over-automating too soon** - Start with 1-2 key reports

2. **Not reviewing the automation** - Check quarterly for needed updates

3. **Ignoring the human element** - Add your insights to the raw numbers

4. **Forgetting mobile users** - Ensure reports look good on phones

Your Action Plan

1. **Pick one report** to automate this week

2. **Choose the right tool** for your needs

3. **Build a prototype** and test it

4. **Schedule deliveries** to key stakeholders

5. **Refine over time** based on feedback

Remember: The goal isn't just to save time - it's to have better data at your fingertips so you can make smarter decisions faster.

In our next lesson, we'll explore how to turn these reports into actual strategy improvements. But first, get one automated report running - that first Monday morning when it magically appears in your inbox will feel like Christmas.

Pro tip: Name your automated reports clearly (like "Q3 Marketing Performance - Auto") so everyone knows they're looking at the latest numbers.

Lesson 3: Using Data for Continuous Improvement

Let me tell you about a coffee shop owner named Maria who nearly doubled her business in six months without increasing her marketing budget. Her secret? She stopped guessing what customers wanted and started letting the data guide her decisions. When she noticed iced drinks sold better in the morning than afternoon, she shifted her promotions. When loyalty data showed certain customers only came in on weekends, she created a weekday special just for them. This is the power of data-driven optimization we're going to unlock for you.

Moving Beyond Surface-Level Metrics

Most marketers look at the same basic stats every day - clicks, opens, conversions. But the real gold comes from connecting the dots between these numbers to spot trends and patterns. Here's what you should really be tracking:

Customer Journey Patterns

- What paths do converters take versus non-converters?

- Where do high-value customers first engage with you?

- What content actually leads to sales versus just engagement?

Time-Based Trends

- How does performance fluctuate by day/hour?

- Are there seasonal patterns you're missing?

- How does customer behavior change throughout the week?

Audience Insights

- Which segments have the highest lifetime value?

- What unexpected demographics are engaging?

- How do different age groups interact with your content?

Turning Insights Into Action

Spotting trends is useless unless you do something with them. Here's how to make data actionable:

If you notice...

- Certain products sell better at specific times → Adjust your ad scheduling

- Mobile users convert at half the rate of desktop → Optimize your mobile experience

- Email open rates drop after 2 PM → Change your send times

- A particular ad creative outperforms others → Make more content in that style

Real Example:

An online course creator noticed students who watched at least 3 lessons in the first week were 5x more likely to complete the course. So she:

1. Created an automated email sequence for students who stalled after Lesson 1

2. Added bonus content after Lesson 3 to boost momentum

3. Adjusted her ads to target learners with similar engagement patterns

Result: Course completion rates increased by 62%.

Building Your Optimization Process

1. **Weekly Trend Review**

   o Pick 1-2 key metrics to analyze deeply

   o Look for 3-month patterns, not just weekly fluctuations

   o Document potential causes for changes

2. **Monthly Experiment Planning**

- Based on trends, choose 1 hypothesis to test

- Example: "If we change our checkout page layout, conversions will increase"

- Set clear success metrics before starting

3. **Quarterly Strategy Pivot**

- Review all accumulated data

- Identify what's working/not working

- Adjust your marketing mix accordingly

Tools That Help

Google Analytics Annotations
Mark campaign launches and external events to contextualize data changes

Hotjar Recordings
Watch real user sessions to understand behavior

Microsoft Clarity
Free heatmaps and session recordings

Google Optimize
Run A/B tests without coding

Avoiding Analysis Paralysis

It's easy to get stuck in "just one more report" mode. Remember:

- Focus on trends that last at least 2-3 weeks

- Prioritize metrics tied to revenue

- Set time limits for analysis sessions

- Implement first, perfect later

Your Action Plan

1. **Pick one campaign** to analyze deeply this week

2. **Identify one surprising trend** in the data

3. **Form one hypothesis** about why it's happening

4. **Make one change** to test your theory

5. **Measure the impact** over 2-4 weeks

The companies that win aren't those with the most data - they're the ones who use data to make better decisions faster. Start small, but start today.

In our capstone project, we'll bring all these lessons together. But first, try analyzing one customer journey from start to finish - you'll likely find at least one "why didn't we see this before?" moment.

Pro tip: Keep an "insights journal" where you document your observations and the actions you took. Over time, you'll see patterns in what types of optimizations work best for your business.

Hands-On: Build Your First Data-Driven Marketing Report

Let's cut through the theory—by the end of this task, you'll have a real, actionable report that highlights **what's working, what's not**, and **where to improve** in your marketing. No fluff, just a step-by-step guide to turn raw data into smart decisions.

Step 1: Pick a Campaign to Analyze

Choose **one** recent marketing effort to evaluate, such as:

- ☑ A Facebook/Google Ads campaign
- ☑ An email marketing sequence
- ☑ A social media promotion
- ☑ A content marketing push

Not sure? Pick the campaign where you're **least certain** about its performance.

Step 2: Gather Your Data

Pull key metrics from:

- **Google Analytics** (traffic, conversions, bounce rate)

- **Ads platforms** (CTR, CPC, ROAS)

- **Email/Social tools** (open rates, engagement)

- **CRM/Sales data** (revenue, customer acquisition cost)

Pro tip: Use **Google Data Studio** or **Power BI** to connect these sources automatically.

Step 3: Structure Your Report

Keep it simple but insightful. Use this template:

1. Campaign Summary

- Goal (e.g., "Increase signups by 20%")

- Timeframe (e.g., "June 1-30, 2023")

- Budget vs. actual spend

2. Key Performance Metrics

- **Traffic:** Sessions, sources

- **Engagement:** CTR, time on page

- **Conversions:** Leads, sales, ROAS

- **Cost Efficiency:** CPA, CPC

Visualize trends with simple charts (bar graphs for comparisons, line charts for trends).

3. Top Insights

Spot **3-5 key takeaways**, like:
✓ "Video ads outperformed static images by 35%."
✓ "Email subject lines with emojis had 22% higher opens."
✗ "Mobile traffic converted 50% less than desktop."

4. Opportunities for Improvement

Based on the data, suggest **2-3 actionable optimizations**, such as:

- "Test more video ads in the next campaign."

- "Optimize checkout flow for mobile users."

- "Increase budget for high-ROAS ad sets."

Step 4: Automate Future Reports

Save time by setting up **auto-updating dashboards**:

- **Google Looker Studio**: Connect GA, Ads, and social metrics → Schedule weekly emails.

- **Power BI**: Blend CRM + ad data → Share live dashboards with your team.

Real-World Example

A SaaS company analyzed their LinkedIn ad campaign and discovered:

- **Top performer:** Carousel ads (2X more conversions than single images).

- **Weak spot:** Landing page had a 70% drop-off rate.

- **Action taken:** Redesigned the landing page and doubled ad spend on carousels.

- **Result:** 40% lower CPA in the next month.

Final Tips

◆ **Focus on trends, not one-off numbers** (e.g., "CTR dropped every weekend").

◆ **Compare against benchmarks** (industry standards or past campaigns).

◆ **Keep it concise** — 1-2 pages max.

Time needed: ~60-90 mins for your first report (much faster once automated).

Done? Congrats! You've just moved from guessing to **data-driven marketing.** 🚀

Next step: Share your report with your team and plan **one optimization** to test.

(Stuck? Google "[Your Tool] + report template" — most platforms have ready-made examples!)

Capstone Project: Your Automated Marketing Campaign Blueprint

Alright, let's roll up our sleeves and put everything we've learned into action. This is where you'll design your own marketing automation system from scratch - something that actually works while you sleep. I'll walk you through creating a complete plan, then analyzing the results like a pro.

Step 1: Choose Your Campaign Battlefield

Pick one area to automate first (don't overcomplicate it):

- **Email Series** (Welcome sequence, abandoned cart)

- **Social Media** (Content calendar + engagement)

- **Paid Ads** (Facebook/Google automated campaigns)

- **Full Funnel** (Combining several channels)

Stuck? Go with what's currently eating up most of your time.

Step 2: Build Your Automation Framework

Use this simple structure:

1. Goal Setting

- What exactly should this campaign achieve?

- How will you measure success?

2. Tool Selection

- Pick 1-2 main platforms (Mailchimp, HubSpot, etc.)

- Choose complementary apps (Zapier for connections)

3. Workflow Design

- Map out every step from first contact to conversion

- Identify repetitive tasks to automate

- Set up if-this-then-that rules

4. Personalization Plan

- How will you tailor messages?

- What triggers different paths?

5. Reporting Setup

- Which metrics matter most?

- How often will you check in?

Step 3: Implementation Checklist

Here's how to actually build it:

☑ For Email Campaigns:

- Set up segmentation rules

- Create automated response triggers

- Design A/B test templates

✅ **For Social Media:**

- Connect your scheduling tool

- Build a content repository

- Set up engagement responders

✅ **For Paid Ads:**

- Enable auto-bidding strategies

- Create AI-optimized audiences

- Set performance alerts

Step 4: Your Analysis Playbook

After it runs for 2-4 weeks, dig into:

The Good

- What outperformed expectations?

- Which automations saved the most time?

The Bad

- Where did the system fall short?

- What needed manual intervention?

The Unexpected

- Surprising customer behaviors

- Unintended consequences

Step 5: Optimization Plan

Based on your findings:

1. **Double down** on what worked

2. **Fix or replace** what didn't

3. **Test one big improvement**

4. **Document everything** for next time

Real-World Example: Local Bakery Automation

What They Automated:

- Instagram post scheduling

- Facebook Messenger order inquiries

- Email follow-ups after purchases

Results After 60 Days:

- Saved 12 hours/week on manual tasks

- Increased repeat orders by 35%

- Grew social following by 20%

Their Key Insight:

Automating order confirmations led to fewer customer service calls about order status.

Your Turn: Make It Happen

1. **Start small** - one campaign, one funnel

2. **Build the basics** before adding complexity

3. **Schedule weekly check-ins** (15 mins max)

4. **Tweak one thing at a time**

Remember - perfection isn't the goal. Getting a working system in place is. You can always refine later.

Final Deliverable:

Create a simple 2-page document with:

1. Your automation blueprint

2. Performance analysis

3. Three specific improvements to test next

That's it! You've now got a marketing machine that works while you focus on growing your business. How good does that sound?

Pro tip: Set a calendar reminder to review this in 3 months - you'll be amazed how much you'll improve it by then.

Attachments:

1. Marketing Automation Plan Template

What's Inside:

- Campaign goal-setting worksheet

- Workflow mapping canvas

- Tool selection checklist

- 30/60/90 day rollout plan

- Team responsibility matrix

How To Use It:

Open the PDF, type directly into the blue fields, and you'll have a professional plan ready in 20 minutes. Includes examples from real e-commerce and B2B companies.

2. Automation Tools Comparison Chart

Covers 12 Top Platforms:

Tool	Best For	Pricing	Key Feature	Learning Curve
Mailchimp	Email newbies	0–0–299/mo	Drag-and-drop builder	Low
ActiveCampaign	Advanced automation	29–29–259/mo	Conditional logic	Medium

HubSpot	All-in-one	0-0-3,200/mo	CRM integration	High
...plus 9 others with honest pros/cons				

Bonus: Includes our "If You're [X], Choose [Y]" recommendations for different business types.

3. Performance Report Kit

3 Ready-To-Use Templates:

1. **Executive Summary** (1-pager for leadership)

2. **Team Deep Dive** (5-7 page detailed analysis)

3. **Test Result Report** (A/B test documentation)

Each comes with:

- Sample data showing how to interpret numbers

- Conditional formatting rules

- Data visualization best practices

- Automated Google Sheets version available

4. Real Campaign Case Studies

7 Proven Examples:

1. E-commerce: How a $200K/month store automated 80% of their marketing

2. Local Service: Plumbing company's chatbot that books $15K/month in appointments

3. SaaS: Automated onboarding sequence that reduced churn by 40%

4. ...plus 4 others across industries

Each case study breaks down:

- Before/after metrics

- Exact workflows used

- Screenshots of actual automations

- Lessons learned

How To Get The Most From These:

1. **Start with the template** - Even filling out just the first page will give you clarity

2. **Reference the tool chart** when feeling overwhelmed by options

3. **Use the reports weekly** - They're designed to save you hours

4. **Steal ideas** from the case studies but adapt them to your needs

These aren't just theoretical documents - they're the same templates we use with our consulting clients (just without the $5,000 price tag). The performance report alone has helped teams cut meeting prep time from 3 hours to 20 minutes.

Pro Tip: Open the case studies first when you're feeling stuck - nothing beats seeing how others solved similar problems.

About the author

Dr. Aziza Tawfiq Abdelghafar, a PhD holder from Ain Shams University, is an expert in strategic planning, marketing, and administrative sciences. With extensive experience in academia, industry, and entrepreneurship, she has authored specialized books and research papers. A sought-after speaker, she has contributed to scientific and industrial conferences, shaping the future of marketing and management sciences.